Challenge your worries one by one

For ages 7–11

With top advice for your grown-up too!

THE WORRY

Grrr!

The Worry Warriors' Activity Book

WORKBOOK

Write on the magic mirror of compliments

Let go of your worries with mindful morsels and tummy balloons

IMOGEN HARRISON
Foreword by **Dr Pooky Knightsmith**

vie

THE WORRY WORKBOOK

An Hachette UK Company
www.hachette.co.uk

Vie Books, an imprint of Summersdale Publishers Ltd
Part of Octopus Publishing Group Limited
Carmelite House
50 Victoria Embankment
LONDON
EC4Y 0DZ
UK

www.summersdale.com

Printed and bound in China

ISBN: 978-1-78783-537-5

Substantial discounts on bulk quantities of Summersdale books are available to corporations, professional associations and other organizations. For details contact general enquiries: telephone: +44 (0) 1243 771107 or email: enquiries@summersdale.com.

Neither the author nor the publisher can be held responsible for any loss or claim arising out of the use, or misuse, of the suggestions made herein. None of the views or suggestions in this book is intended to replace medical opinion from a doctor. If you have concerns about your health or that of a child in your care, please seek professional advice.

This book belongs to...

_____

Contents

FOREWORD

by Dr Pooky Knightsmith

The regular worries that all children experience day-to-day are a brilliant learning opportunity for how to manage "Big Stuff" later on. By building their ability to understand worries and developing their skills and confidence in taming their worries and managing their feelings, we give them a brilliant toolkit for life.

The Worry Workbook is a fabulous springboard for this learning, with simple, fun activities that children will readily engage with, which will help them to understand what's worrying them and what they can do about it.

There is also clear guidance for us supporting adults about what we can do to help too; though often just tagging along for the journey with listening ears and a kind heart is the most important job of all.

This is an ideal resource for every child and one that has the full endorsement of my own worry warriors, Lyra and Ellie who, like all children, need to learn that worries are normal and healthy, but we don't have to let them control us; we can fight back, take control and win the worry war!

Welcome,
parents and carers!

This book is designed to help you and your child work through their worries in a fun and accessible way, as well as being a learning tool to understanding how and why worry happens.

We all worry, and your child is not alone in feeling this way — worry is a normal part of a healthy emotional life, so eradicating it completely is neither possible nor desirable. The aim is to give your child the tools to deal with normal levels of worry, and to know how to recognize and ask for help if it becomes too much. This way, you are setting them up to be emotionally strong and mentally resilient for life.

You know your child best and you may choose to work with them on the activities, but let them speak, and be careful not to influence their responses. The best way to support them is through active listening so that your child feels safe expressing themselves to you. Let them have their say and respond by using body language to show you are listening and

8

understanding. When the moment's right, paraphrase what they have said, showing they have your full attention. You don't need to agree with your child — a lot of worries can be irrational — but you can still affirm and empathize with them.

If your child would prefer not to write down or discuss specific thoughts, the same themes in the book can be explored through drawing and painting, role-playing games, building blocks, singing songs, dancing to music or making mud pies — whatever captures your child's imagination. Research has found expressing difficult emotions through creative play is one of the most effective ways for children to process their feelings and improve their mental health.

Look out for the parent/carer and child icons, as these act as signposts for more technical information about the relevance and usefulness of a specific activity.

There is further content for parents and carers at the end of the book.

I hope this book is a positive and fun journey for you and your child.

HELLO!

Welcome to your new anti-worry activity book. This is not your average activity book because it's not only HEAPS OF FUN but it will also teach you some AMAZING LIFE SKILLS to help you take control of your worries. It's not nice feeling worried — and the thing about worry is that it can stop you from having fun and being happy in your everyday life.

**Here are some questions to ask yourself:
Do you often...**

- **Miss out on fun stuff because you worry?**

- **Have worries in your head that won't go away?**

- **Feel tired from worrying too much?**

- **Feel unconfident about being away from your grown-up?**

If you are nodding your head while reading the list, then you have come to the right place. It's time to get stuck in and find your way to beating your worries with fun challenges and activities, including unlocking and decluttering your worry cabinet, growing brain spaghetti, visiting the magic mirror of compliments, blowing tummy balloons and sampling mindful morsels, and so much more.

At the end of this book, you will have your own unique WORRY SHRINKER, a special list of things that work for you to make your worries shrink so they're either teeny-tiny or completely invisible. Sounds good, doesn't it?

Take your grown-up along for the ride, because there are special tips throughout for them to read with you if you want, and some of the activities are even more fun if your grown-up does them too! Look for this icon for the special tips.

Are you ready? Then turn the page...

TALKING ABOUT IT

Write down your three favourite and most trusted grown-ups that you feel you can call upon to talk through your worries. You could even draw in their faces!

Name: _____

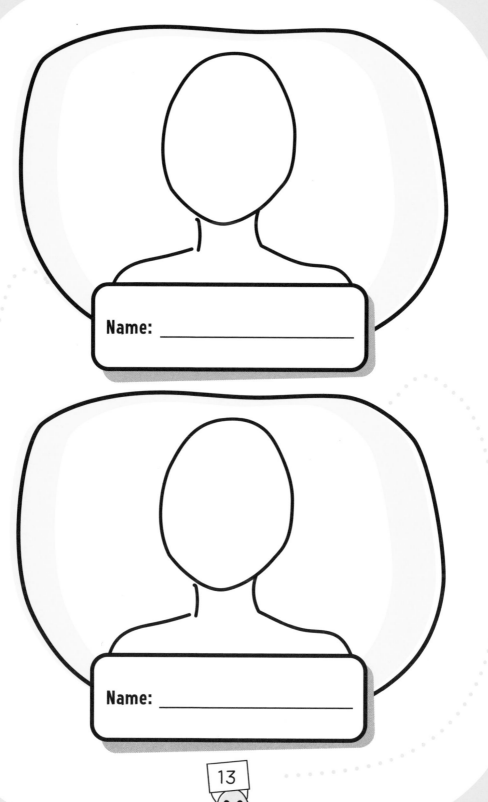

Name: _____

Name: _____

WHAT IS WORRYING ALL ABOUT?

Everyone has their very own inner alarm system that goes off when danger seems close by. It's called the fight-or-flight response, but there is also a third response: freeze. The fight-or-flight response was very valuable 300,000 years ago when you might suddenly meet a sabre-toothed tiger, but life-and-death situations such as that aren't as common today, thankfully! Despite this, your alarm system is still ready to go off at the merest sign of threat, and it can strike at any time.

Grrrr!

When we start to worry, we typically experience one of three physical responses:

1 – FIGHT: a rush of energy in your body; the tensing muscles and rapid heart rate is designed to sharpen your senses to take on that sabre-toothed tiger.

2 – FLIGHT: the same burst of energy prepares you to run away from the sabre-toothed tiger and seek safety.

3 – FREEZE: this is the response when you have seen the sabre-toothed tiger and you stay perfectly still in the hope that it hasn't spotted you.

Worrying is so normal

If you were faced with something really scary what would you do? Fight, take flight, or freeze? Read the scenarios below and tick the box that applies to you.

You're about to leave the house to go to school, but you suddenly feel nervous about a test later that day as you've convinced yourself you won't be able to answer anything, and you start to feel a bit unwell.	FIGHT ☐ FLIGHT ☐ FREEZE ☐	
You suddenly feel hot and nervous when the teacher asks you to read a passage of text to the class.	FIGHT ☐ FLIGHT ☐ FREEZE ☐	

It's your turn to do show and tell, your mouth dries up and you're feeling really worried that you'll lose your voice.

FIGHT ☐
FLIGHT ☐
FREEZE ☐

You worry about seeing a particular friend again because you had a disagreement the last time you saw them and think they might make you feel sad.

FIGHT ☐
FLIGHT ☐
FREEZE ☐

These sorts of worries are completely normal. It's important to remember that everyone has worries and you're not alone in feeling like this.

The exercises in this book will provide the tools to help you train your brain out of worrying on a regular basis.

The feeling we have in our bodies during the fight-or-flight response is caused by adrenaline. Adrenaline is a hormone that is released when we feel strong emotions, such as worry, fear or excitement, and it exists to protect us from danger by making us feel strong and powerful.

HOW WORRY AFFECTS YOUR BODY

Here's a list of feelings that
you might experience when your
fight-or-flight alarm goes off.

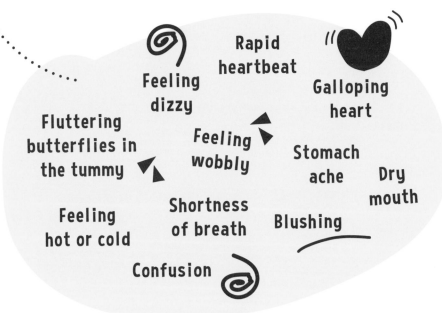

Feeling
dizzy

Rapid
heartbeat

Galloping
heart

Fluttering
butterflies in
the tummy

Feeling
wobbly

Stomach
ache

Dry
mouth

Feeling
hot or cold

Shortness
of breath

Blushing

Confusion

None of these symptoms sound very nice, do they?
But it's important to recognize how you feel when you're
worried, so you can begin to take steps to ease these
symptoms. Then you'll be able to help your
inner alarm realize that you're not about to
be devoured by a sabre-toothed tiger.

Grrrr!

18

Draw your face and favourite clothes onto the outline. Then, look at the list and circle the feelings that you experience when you worry and colour these points in red on the body.

FIVE-DAY CHALLENGE

Find out what makes your fight-or-flight alarm ring once and for all!

Now that you know what feelings to look out for when your fight-or-flight alarm goes off, it's time to make a record of when it rings. By doing some simple detective work, you will find out what it is that makes you worry. And when you know that, you can take steps to stop it from happening.

Use the diary on this page — fill in the spaces and record the time, the situation you were in when your alarm rang, and how you felt.

	Time	Situation	How it made me feel
DAY 1			
DAY 2			
DAY 3			
DAY 4			
DAY 5			

20

When you have completed your table, it's time to look over it to see if there are any patterns occurring, for example, does your alarm go off at a certain time of day, in a certain place, or when you are with a certain person?
Write your findings in the alarm-shaped circle below.

EMOTIONAL AWARENESS

Emotional awareness means knowing how you are feeling. Sometimes it's hard to name how we feel — there are so many different emotions, such as CARING when we are stroking a pet, ANGRY when something seems unfair, SCARED if we hear thunder outside, HAPPY after a birthday party, EXCITED about going on a school trip.

Take a look at the jellybeans in the jar. Let's imagine that each one is a different emotion instead of a different flavour! How many emotions can you think of? Some are filled in already. Ask a grown-up to help.

You can keep adding to this page when you think of more emotions.

22

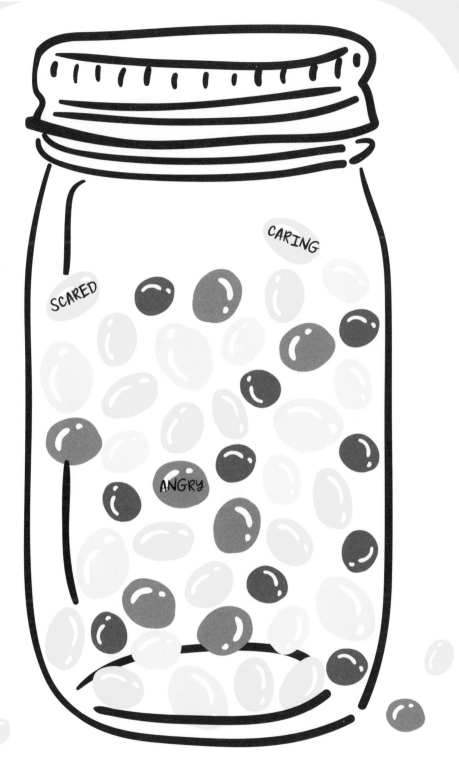

Myself

Colouring in is a very good hobby to have if you worry a lot because it has been proven by scientists to be as relaxing as meditation. This is because it makes your mind switch off the worries in your head in order to focus on colouring.

THE WORRY CAMERA

The worry camera is a magic camera. It will take a snapshot of how you are feeling at this very moment. It does this by converting your feelings into colours.

Here's what you need to do:

- Pick five of your favourite colours.
- Colour in each star at the bottom of the page so each one is different.
- Label each star with a different feeling – use the list from page 23 to help.
- Colour in the image using the colour key that you have created.

_____   _____   _____   _____   _____

Wow, look how colourful your feelings are!

27

LISTEN TO YOUR THOUGHTS

Your thoughts are very powerful and have a huge effect on how you feel inside. Most of the times that your worry alarm goes off are due to unhelpful thoughts swimming in your head — like the scenario where you **really do** get eaten by an actual sabre-toothed tiger for forgetting your homework.

Your thoughts are almost infinite — they include every memory, every conversation, every fart and burp, every hug, every piece of birthday cake, every laugh with your friends, quite simply everything. Somehow there's still room for thoughts about what might happen, from the next moment, to the next day, to way into the future, to thoughts about things that could never, ever happen. That's a lot of thoughts jostling for your attention. To give you an idea of how many things that is, ask a parent to take you to the top of a hill on a starry night and look up at the sky. See how many stars you can count, then times that by the biggest number you can think of — that's how many thoughts and memories you have. It's a wonder your head isn't the size of a watermelon!

What are you thinking about right now?
Sit quietly and pay attention to your thoughts. Write or
doodle the words and pictures that come to your
mind in the stars on this page.

Self-talk

This is such an important life lesson, so pay attention please!

The constant stream of thoughts that we have just talked about affects how we feel and how we behave, just like this:

THOUGHTS = PHYSICAL FEELINGS = HOW WE BEHAVE

This stream of thoughts is sometimes called "self-talk" or our "inner voice". Your inner voice has immense power — it can make you happy, down in the dumps, fizz with excitement, bad-tempered or really worried, and every other emotion you can think of.

How is your inner voice making you feel right now? Have a look at the thoughts and words that you wrote down in the starry sky on page 29 and then write in the speech bubbles how those things are making you feel.

Thought bubble

The Worry Cabinet

In every person's brain is a worry cabinet. It's where all the things that you worry about lurk and sometimes it can get a bit over-full. Write your worries on the labels; the little drawers are for small everyday worries, and the big drawers are for the things that you worry about the most.

When we write down our worries, it can make them seem less scary. If you work with your grown-up on this activity, it can help you to work out which worries need the most attention, so that you can tackle them together one by one, and find solutions for them.

32

Things you can't control

Once you have finished the worry cabinet, it's time to declutter it. The first thing to do is get rid of the worries that you can't control. It could be things like thunderstorms or something you have heard about on a news programme. See if you can compile a list from your worry drawers of the things you can't control.

Once you realize that these things are out of your hands, it becomes easier to stop worrying about them. For all the other worries, it's time to learn a few strategies to keep those worries at bay...

Sharing your worries with your grown-up can help you to worry less. When it's something you can't control, such as global warming, have a think about what you can do together to help you feel like you're making a positive difference. If the worry is about your family, for example if your grown-up spends a lot of time at work, one solution would be to do more fun activities together when they are at home. If you find it hard to talk about your worry, it can help to use toys in a role-play scenario so you can feel like the problem is separate to yourself.

35

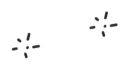

Tizzy Fizzy

Your all-too-efficient fight-or-flight alarm creates adrenaline — which in turn causes all those unpleasant physical feelings that we'll refer to as the Tizzy Fizzy.

Here's a glass of the most delicious fizzy drink. Guess what? It's called Tizzy Fizzy. Pick a situation that makes you worry. Write it down on the drinks coaster under the drink. Now fill in the bubbles with the feelings that this situation makes you have. The bigger the bubble, the bigger the feeling.

The fight-or-flight alarm lives in a section of your brain called the amygdala. This primitive part of your brain likes to act rather than think, which is why adrenaline is produced so quickly when we worry. The adrenaline, the tizzy fizzy, gives you all of those unpleasant feelings that we talked about on page 18.

POSITIVE SELF-TALK: HOW TO LOOK ON THE BRIGHT SIDE

See how amazingly powerful your thoughts are?
Once you know that your thoughts affect your mood and
how you feel physically, you can change how you feel just
by changing your thoughts! The next few activities will
show you how to build your positive self-talk skills.

Positive self-talk is when we talk kindly to ourselves
in a reassuring and helpful way. For example,
imagine you received the results for a school test
and perhaps you didn't do as well as you'd hoped.

It's easy to say to yourself, "Silly me,
I should have done better."

But a more reassuring and optimistic thing to say
to yourself would be, "I did the best I could that
day and it's OK to make mistakes. I will keep trying
and next time I know I will do so much better."

Saying and thinking nice things about
yourself will give you a big confidence
boost. If you do it every day, it can make
you worry less as well as improve
your overall health and well-being. It's
important for grown-ups to do it too!

Feel-good statements

Here's a list of positive self-talk statements that you might like to say to yourself:

There is no one better to be than myself

I forgive myself for my mistakes

I am an amazing person

My mistakes help me learn and grow

I am loved

40

I deserve
to be
happy

Today
I am going
to shine

I have
courage
and
confidence

**No matter
how hard
it is, I
can do it**

I can be
anything
I want
to be

I can make a
difference

The magic mirror of compliments

Imagine you were meeting yourself. What nice things would you say about what you're good at and your talents? What compliments would you give about your values, manners or appearance?

Write your ten nicest compliments to yourself in the mirror.

1.

2.

3.

4.

5.

6.

7.

8.

9.

10.

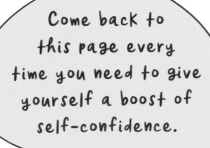

Come back to this page every time you need to give yourself a boost of self-confidence.

It feels good to appreciate yourself and recognize that you're pretty awesome!

Once you have finished your list, look in a real mirror and say these great compliments to yourself.

When you have your list of ten compliments — grown-ups too — you can say them out loud to yourself every morning to set you up for the day. You might feel a bit silly to begin with as you say them out loud, but it's essential to do this in order to challenge and change any negative thinking in your head.

I'm PROUD

The five-day bright-side challenge

Over the course of the next five days, every time you catch your inner voice speaking negatively, write down what the negative inner voice is saying on this page. Then, with your grown-up, think about how you can rephrase the sentence into one that is kind and optimistic. It might seem difficult at first, but here are a few questions you can ask yourself to make it easier:

- **How can I learn from this?**
- **What good thing can I carry with me to help me next time?**
- **What went right?**

It's good to get into the habit of saying nice things to yourself, especially when you experience a disappointment or make a mistake as these are the times when you need the most encouragement to pick yourself up again. Having a positive inner voice when bad stuff happens will make you strong and resilient — this is an important skill to carry with you for your whole life.

	Negative voice	Positive voice
DAY 1		
DAY 2		
DAY 3		
DAY 4		
DAY 5		

GROW YOUR BRAIN!

Feeling worried can stop you from wanting to try new things. Something we haven't done before might make us worry that we'll make mistakes because it seems DIFFICULT or SCARY or maybe even a bit STRANGE. And when the worry alarm goes off it can make you want to shrink away and not try those new things.

But, did you know that every time you try something different or something new, your brain GROWS new connections? These connections are called neural pathways. The more you do the new things the stronger these connections become; for example, you can recite the alphabet with no effort at all, and you can do your three times table because you've done it so many times in maths. These pathways become the norm.

You can apply the same principle to any activity, so the next time you are worried about trying something new, don't think about the possibility of making a mistake, instead think of the new neural pathways being created in your brain!

The best way to encourage each other (you and your grown-up!) to have a growth mindset is to allow yourselves to be overheard when you are "thinking aloud" as you come up with positive ways to approach things that might be new to you. You can do it!

Brain spaghetti!
The pathways game

Imagine this is your brain with all the different pathways joining up and looping around like spaghetti! Over the course of a week, see if you can fill in the gaps with new things that you have tried, then draw the lines by joining up the dots to create pathways and colour them in. This will help you to see how your brain grows bigger and ever more complex every time you try new things.

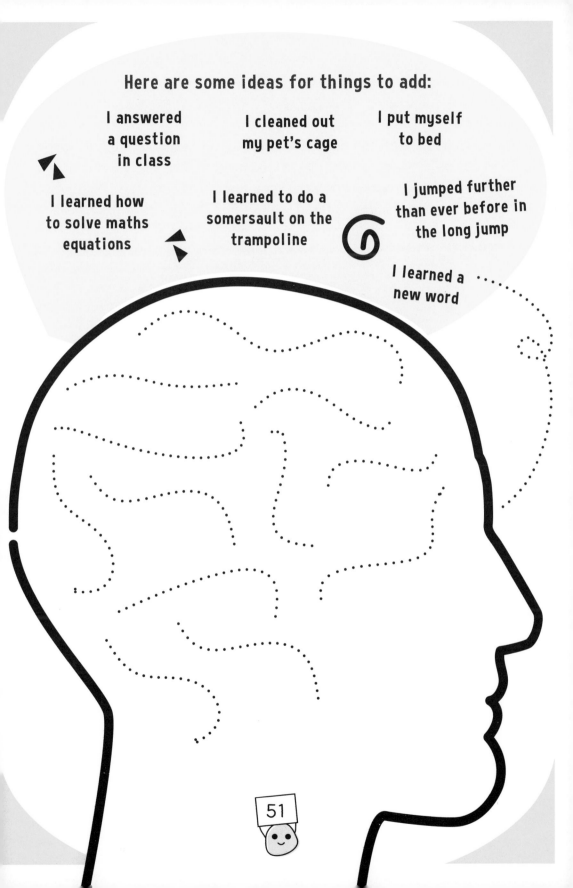

SCRIBBLE DIARY

It can be difficult to know how to explain how you're feeling, so let's try drawing your feelings instead. Use this diary page to draw how you're feeling with just a few lines, dots or scribbles in the course of a day. Make it a day when you're out doing things with your grown-up so you can remind each other to fill it in. Maybe get your grown-up to fill in their own scribble diary too!

Here's an example diary:

You can name your emotions once you have drawn them.

Drawing your emotions helps you to become aware of how you're feeling in the present moment. Try this activity at different times of day. If you're struggling for ideas, talk with your grown-up and think about words that come to mind — they don't have to be specific feelings like "happy" or "sad"; maybe you feel "itchy" or "sunny" or something like that — these words are a window on how you're feeling inside.

Monday	Tuesday	Wednesday	Thursday	Friday	Saturday	Sunday

MAKE YOUR OWN FIDGET SPINNER!

Sometimes when we're worried it helps to focus our mind on an activity. Some people like to kick a ball around or play throw and catch, while others might enjoy colouring in or doing a jigsaw. These activities can be helpful distractions when we start to worry about something, and it teaches your brain that you can overcome worrying thoughts by doing something that you enjoy instead.

Here's a fun thing to make and play with to help soothe you when you're feeling worried. It's also pocket size so you can take it out and about.

Have a few favourite activities ready for those times when you start to feel worried. It could be reading a comic or drawing in a sketchbook. These fun things will help to distract you from your worries.

Make a simple fidget spinner by carefully copying the spinner template below onto card and cutting it out.

Use a hole punch to punch out the three holes on the limbs. Ask a grown-up to make a hole in the centre of the spinner for a split pin.

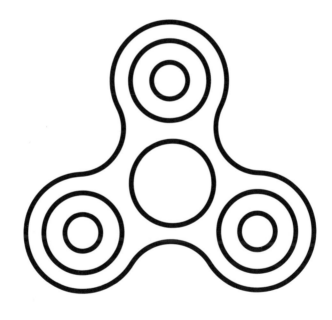

HAPPY TIME!

These are the happy pages — only smiles are allowed round here. This is THE place to go to whenever you're feeling worried.

Fill it with all the things that make you happy and give you a lift. Here are some ideas for things you could add:

Pictures of your family, friends or pets

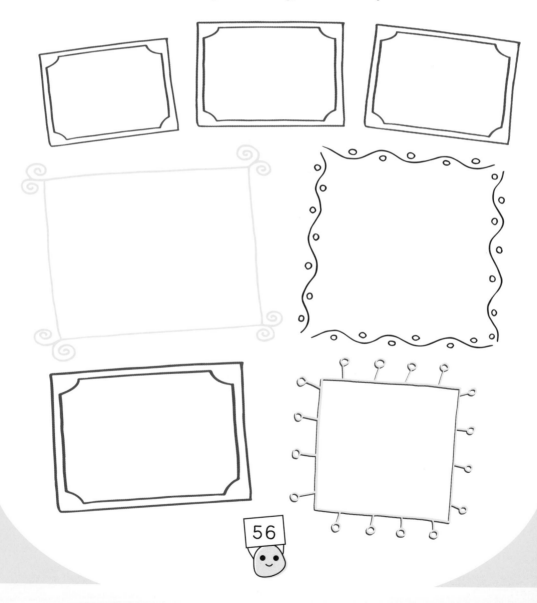

Funny jokes

Draw your favourite fancy dress outfit

HAPPY TIME!

Silly words

Memories of your favourite
holiday or days out

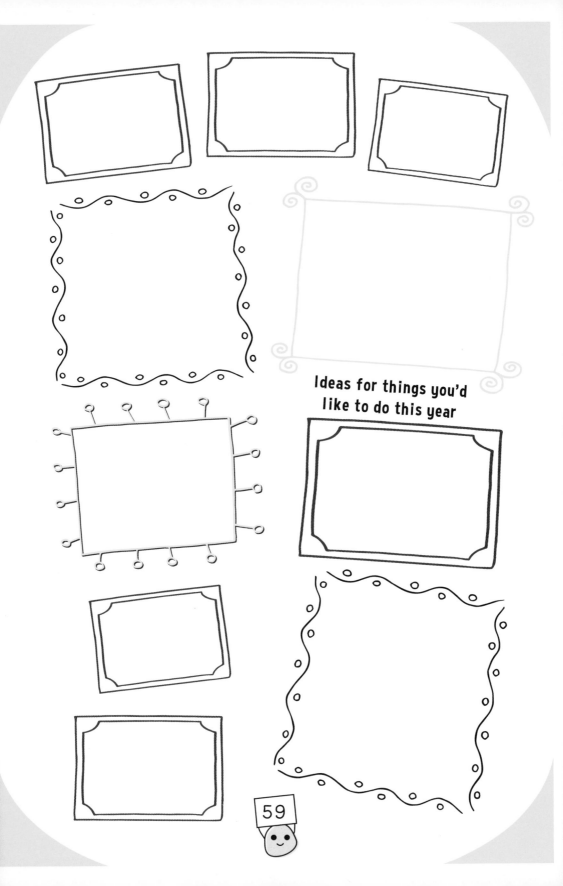

Ideas for things you'd like to do this year

GET BUSY!

Physical exercise raises the heart rate and burns away excess adrenaline, the "tizzy fizzy". And just like laughter (see page 96), it also releases something called endorphins into your body, which make you feel happy. Physical exercise doesn't just keep you physically fit and healthy, but also keeps your mind healthy too. What this means is by playing some sport every day, you are less likely to struggle with worry. Here are some exercises to try out — see which ones you like best.

Trampolining

Riding a bike

Yoga

Playing "it"

Running

Swimming

Ball games

Skipping

Any physical exercise that raises your heart rate is good for your health and helps you to worry less. This is because exercise burns away excess adrenaline in your body, making it less likely that you will experience those uncomfortable feelings when faced with a challenging situation.

Time for a stretch

Yoga is very calming as it gently stretches your body. It's also great for helping you sit up straight and pay attention in class as well as standing tall so you feel more confident. It also makes you happy by reducing worry and balancing your mood.

Practising yoga from an early age encourages positive self-esteem and body awareness with a physical activity that's non-competitive.

Yoga also has numerous health benefits and enhances flexibility, strength and coordination. It also improves concentration and promotes a sense of calmness and relaxation.

Here are some simple yoga poses to try. Try to stay in each pose for ten seconds — it's harder than you think! Have a yoga mat or comfy rug or blanket to lie on, and wear comfortable clothes, like a tracksuit or shorts and a top.

MOUNTAIN POSE

Stand with your feet parallel and slightly apart
so that you can balance your weight evenly between
your feet. Stretch your arms up to the sky!

HAPPY BABY POSE

Lie on your back and fold your knees so that they are touching your chest. Keep your knees where they are and stretch your feet up to the ceiling. Reach up between your knees with your hands and hold your feet. Now rock gently like a happy baby.

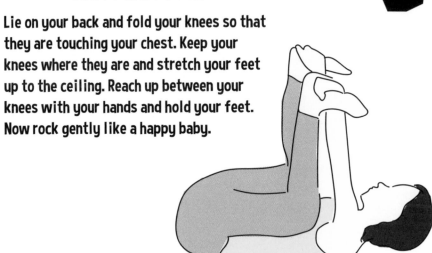

CAT POSE

Begin on your hands and knees, and make your back as flat as possible, like a table top. Make sure your hips are directly above your knees and your arms are straight, like table legs. Breathe out and round your back like a cat, and tuck in your head a little. Now breathe in and return to a flat back.

EASY POSE

This is a pose that you are probably quite familiar with. Sit on the floor and cross your legs, making sure the outer edges of your feet are resting on the floor. Breathe out as you straighten your spine – this is easier to do if you can imagine an invisible thread being pulled from the top of your head. Take a few breaths in this pose and feel your spine lengthening each time you breathe out. You can rest your hands in your lap or on your knees, with your palms facing up.

BRIDGE POSE

Lie on your back and stretch out with your arms to your sides. Bend your knees and place your feet on the floor. Now breathe out and lift your bottom off the floor and tuck in your chin. Try to hold the pose for a few seconds before gently lowering your bottom back onto the floor when you next breathe out.

Activity tracker

It's time to see how being active every day affects your mood and worry levels.

Here's a tracker to record your exercise over the next five days — only write in the times when you can feel your heart rate has been raised as this shows that the exercise has been effective.

After each entry, perhaps give an idea of how you feel, using different forms of smiley face — see the example below to start you off. At the end of the week make a note of your favourite activities as a reminder to do them to make you feel good!

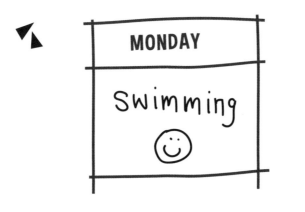

MONDAY

Swimming
☺

MONDAY	TUESDAY	WEDNESDAY	THURSDAY	FRIDAY

My favourite activites are:

_____

LETTING GO OF WORRIES WITH MINDFULNESS

When we feel worried, our fight-or-flight alarm is on high alert. We can feel tense and uncomfortable in our head and in our body. It can help to learn some simple ways to calm yourself when worry strikes, and some of the best ways involve practising mindfulness.

Mindfulness means giving your full attention to something, taking your time and being calm. Practising mindfulness can have many positive effects on how you feel. Here's a list of its magical benefits:

It can make you worry less

It helps you to slow down and make fewer mistakes

It can make you feel more relaxed about chatting to other people

It improves your learning skills because it helps to increase your attention span

It improves your listening

It makes you enjoy things a whole lot more

It's also a fun thing to do with your grown-up and a skill that you can carry with you for your whole life

Wow!

Try the simple mindfulness exercises with your grown-up on the following pages.

MINDFULNESS EXERCISE 1:
FOUR SENSES

This is as simple as it sounds. The idea is to sit quietly and notice four things around you.

Sit with your grown-up on a comfy sofa or rug.

Each person takes it in turns to tell the other person something that they can:

SEE

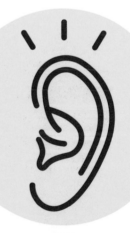

HEAR

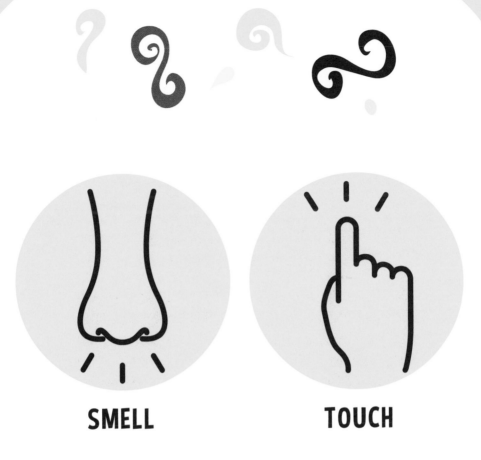

SMELL   **TOUCH**

Make this a regular game to play — a good time
is before bed or walking to or from school.

The next time you feel worried, try the four senses
game and see if it helps you to relax.

MINDFULNESS EXERCISE 2:
THE LISTENING GAME

We have all played the quiet game before – where you try to be silent for as long as you can. This is slightly different, as you need to concentrate on what you can "hear" as well as being silent and still. Play it with your grown-up at home. They can set a timer for one minute. While you're being silent for one minute, see how many different noises you can hear – even the really quiet ones like the creak of a floorboard in another room, or a bird on a branch outside the window.

When your grown-up tells you that the minute is up, see how many things you can recall that you heard and recount them. To make it even more fun, you could both play and write your findings down on a piece of paper once the time is up and see who has heard the most individual noises.

This exercise is a great way for you and
your grown-up to connect in a different way
and will help you to build tools to centre yourself
when you feel stressed or out of sorts.

MINDFULNESS EXERCISE 3:
STAND TALL LIKE A TREE

A great way to calm yourself when you're feeling worried is to stand tall like a tree. It's fun to do this outside in the garden or a park, and even more fun when a group of you do it together to make a forest!

Stand still with your feet slightly apart.

Take a deep breath in through your nose, count to four and breathe out, then do the same again until the end of the exercise.

Each time you breathe out imagine roots growing from your feet deep into the ground.

Stretch out your arms like great branches.

Lengthen your fingers into new growth and imagine leaves sprouting.

Imagine the wind blowing through your branches while you remain still and calm.

74

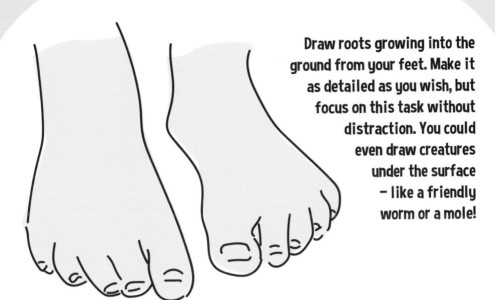

Draw roots growing into the ground from your feet. Make it as detailed as you wish, but focus on this task without distraction. You could even draw creatures under the surface — like a friendly worm or a mole!

MINDFULNESS EXERCISE 4: TUMMY BALLOON

Five breaths to feeling calm

Mindful breathing is one of the simplest ways to help you feel calm and relaxed. It also helps you to focus on the present moment rather than worrying about something in the future.

1

Stand still with your feet slightly apart. Look down at your tummy and place your hand on it.

2

Now breathe in and watch and feel your tummy inflate like a balloon.

5

Repeat the process for four more breaths and see if you can make your tummy balloon a little bigger each time.

3

Hold your breath to the count of three (if you can!).

4

Then exhale slowly and feel your tummy shrink.

6

There are many ways to make mindful breathing simple and fun, just experiment until you find your favourite.

MINDFULNESS EXERCISE 5:
DOODLE BREATHING

Pick up a pen or pencil and take it for a walk by tracing the wavy lines across the page. The important difference – your breath must guide your drawing so the speed of your breathing matches the speed of your drawing.

Try some slow deep breaths and place your pencil or pen tip at the start point.

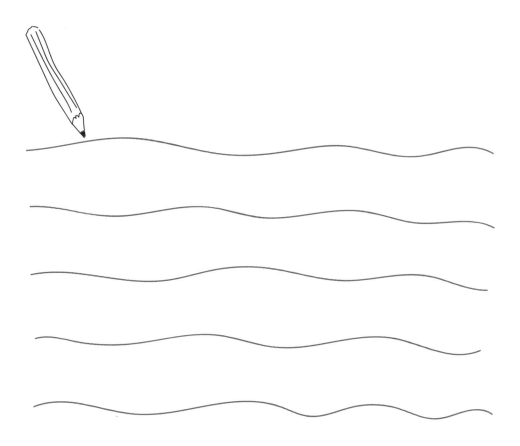

Now inhale as you go up the wave and exhale
as you go down, being careful to match the
movement of the pen to your slow breaths.

You will see that the wavy lines get slightly more
pronounced as you go down the page. So by the time you
reach the last line you should be more relaxed than when
you started and able to inhale and exhale for longer.

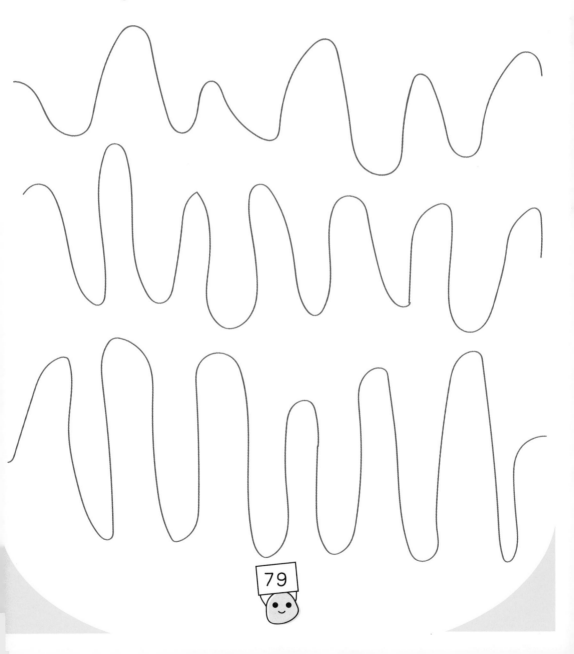

MINDFULNESS EXERCISE 6:
DOODLE AND DAUB

Use these pages to sketch or draw out some doodles using the shapes provided. What do you see? Maybe an animal with three heads, an overflowing letterbox, or perhaps a constellation of stars?

Concentrate fully on your doodles
and enjoy the sense of calm that
creating them brings.

I feel CALM

MINDFULNESS EXERCISE 7:
MINDFUL MORSELS

This is a fun mindfulness exercise to try when you're sitting down for a meal with your grown-up or sibling, or even your whole family!

When the food is served and you're ready to start eating, everyone must pick one thing from their plate as their "mindful morsel" which will be the first mouthful of their meal.

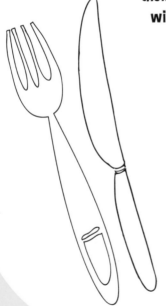

Before you pop your
mindful morsel in your mouth,
have a good look at it, smell it, and
maybe give it a prod with your tongue.
Then place your morsel in your mouth and
slowly chew. Notice how it feels in your
mouth – is it hot or cold, what kind of texture
does it have, and finally, how does it taste?

This can be a fun way to start talking over
the dinner table. Who can come up with
the best descriptive words for
their mindful morsel?

Practising mindfulness with everyday
activities like eating helps you to become
more aware of yourself and your
environment, as well as helping you to
appreciate the joy of everyday life.

You're not a worrier; you're a warrior!

We already know that worrying has nothing to do with personal strength or how courageous you are. We also know that everyone worries, so we're never alone in feeling this way.

Let's switch things up a bit and rethink worry. Don't let worries take over and boss you about because here's the secret: your thoughts don't control you —

YOU CONTROL YOUR THOUGHTS!

Tell your mind it's had its fun, but now you're taking back control — and with the skills you have learnt so far you will be calmer and happier and able to soothe your worries because you are a WARRIOR!

Draw your dream warrior outfit on the body.
Add accessories like super-fast running shoes
to chase away your worries, or super-cool
sunglasses because your future is so bright!

GRATITUDE JOURNAL

Just like the happy pages on page 56, it's important to be able to draw on the things that make you feel good about yourself and your life in general, especially when you might be feeling sad or upset.

Treat the next few pages as a journal to fill in, where you write the three best things that you are grateful for each day. Take a few moments at bedtime to fill it in. It could be something that has happened to you that day, or something kind that someone said to you, or something new you tried that you enjoyed.

Once you have filled the pages, it's nice to look back on all the lovely things in your life, whether they are memories, experiences, people, pets or possessions. See if your grown-up can find you a notebook so you can continue with your gratitude journal. It's a lovely habit to think about good things before going to sleep.

Date: _____

I really appreciate...

_____

_____

_____

Date: _____

I'm particularly grateful for...

_____

_____

_____

Scientific studies show that practising gratitude makes you feel happier. Work with your grown-up and seek out the good things happening around you.

Date: _____

I really appreciate...

_____

_____

_____

Date: _____

I enjoy...

_____

_____

_____

Date: _____

_____

_____

_____

Date:

_____

_____

_____

Date:

_____

_____

_____

Date:

_____

_____

_____

Soothing words activity

What are your favourite words? Which words make you laugh, which ones are puzzling, which ones make you happy or sad? Words are powerful tools to arm yourself with to fight against worry. Calming words can be especially soothing. Some people like to pick a favourite word to think about or say out loud to help them feel calm. These words are called mantras. Fill the kites with your favourite soothing words. Some are filled in already to help you.

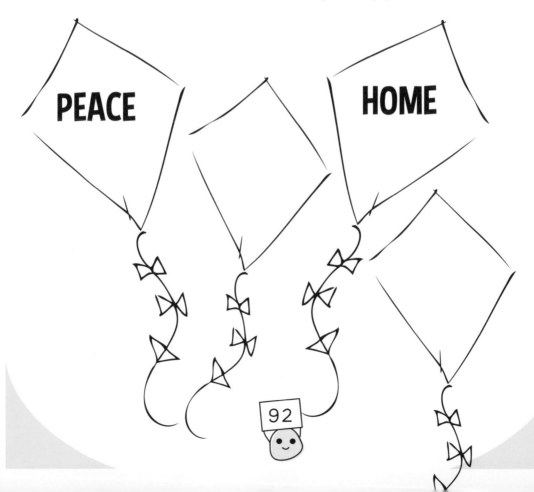

PEACE

HOME

92

You can come back to this
page for a soothing
word whenever
you need it.

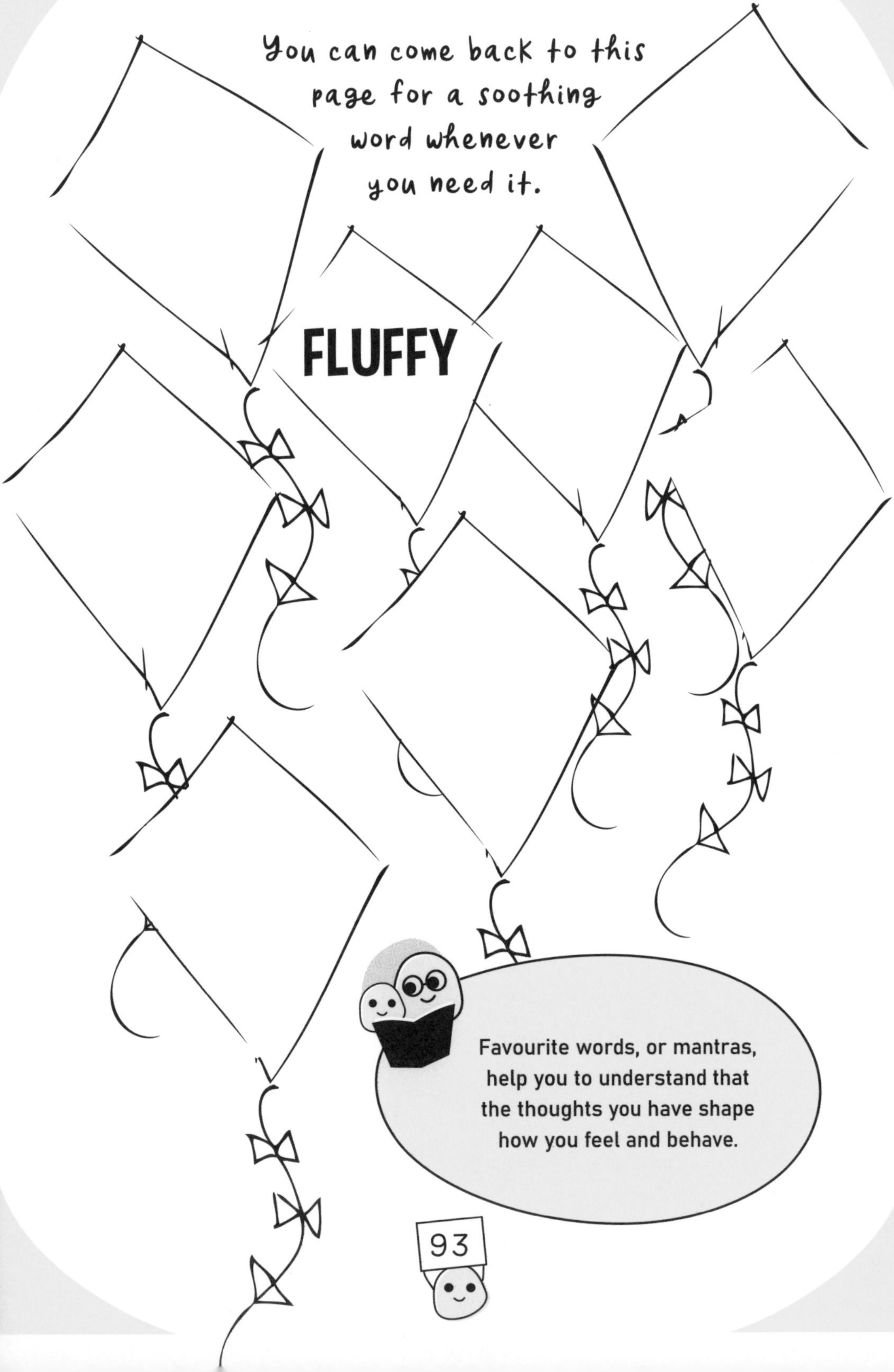

FLUFFY

Favourite words, or mantras,
help you to understand that
the thoughts you have shape
how you feel and behave.

94

Laughter

When was the last time you had a big belly laugh? You know the sort: the ones where your tummy feels like it's going to split from so much laughter. Laughing produces chemicals called endorphins that are released into the bloodstream, and they make you feel happy and stop you from feeling worried. That's not to suggest that you should burst out laughing whenever you feel worried, but a little laughter every day is a very good thing.

Here are some jokes that are guaranteed to tickle your funny bone — test them out on your grown-up too!

How do you make antifreeze?

Steal her pyjamas.

How do snowmen get to work?

By icicle.

What kind of shoes do frogs like?

Open toad sandals.

Doctor, doctor, what do you recommend for flat feet?

Try a foot pump.

Why did the student say his marks were "underwater"?

Because they were below C level.

What is a bear's favourite pasta?

Tagliateddy.

Why did the dog cross the road?

To get to the barking lot.

THE FUNNIEST THING THAT
HAS EVER HAPPENED TO ME...

What comes to mind when you read this sentence? It's time
to recall those moments of hilarity and relive them on this
page with a cartoon strip of images. Here's my funniest
moment on the strip below — don't laugh too hard!

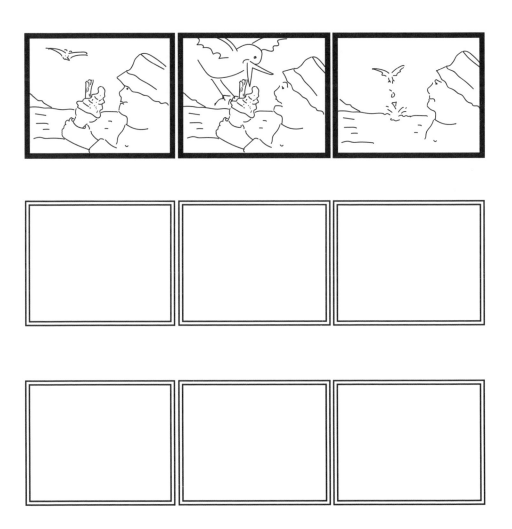

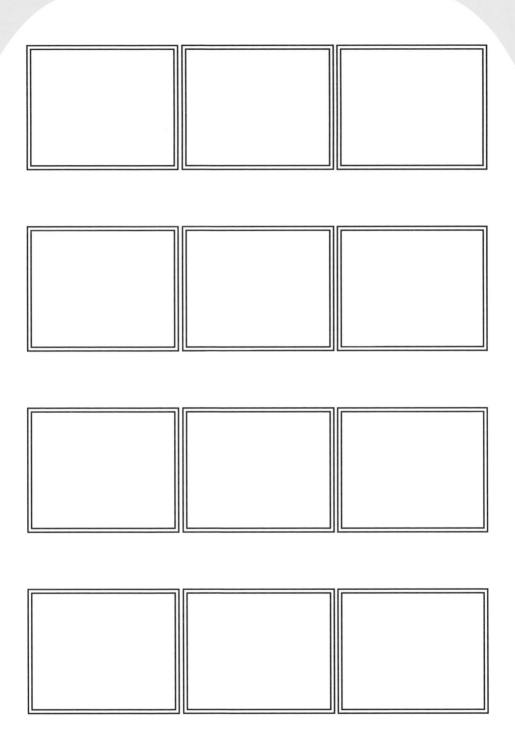

NOW, LET'S TALK ABOUT SLEEP

A good night's sleep is very important to keep you feeling happy and unworried, that's because while you sleep, your body rests and recovers from the day, and your brain processes your thoughts and washes them with a calming solution so you wake up feeling refreshed and ready for the new day.

Sometimes when you're worried it can be difficult to fall asleep, so here are some tips to help you catch those zzzs:

Try to get to bed at the same time every night, so you have the same amount of sleep each night. Bedtime might seem like the dullest part of the day, but you can do some fun calming activities so you actually start to look forward to it!

Have a nice warm bath, preferably with lots of bubbles so you can make bubble beards.

Keep away from screens at
least an hour before bed because
the light from them tricks your
brain into being wide awake.
Instead, get your gratitude journal
out (see page 88) and fill it in.

Read a story with your grown-up. It
could be a whole picture book or a few pages
of a chapter book. According to experts, reading
before bed reduces your worry levels by nearly 70
per cent and helps you have a good night's sleep
– plus you get to explore new worlds and have
fantastic adventures from the comfort
of your cosy bed!

The Sleep Council studies sleep
habits and suggests that a child between
the ages of 7 and 11 needs 10—11 hours' sleep
a night to be able to function well the next day.
Studies have shown that kids who regularly get
an adequate amount of sleep have improved
attention, behaviour, learning, memory, and
overall mental and physical health.

DESIGN YOUR DREAM BEDROOM

Your bedroom should be your happy place, where you can relax. Draw the bedroom of your dreams, a place where you will get the best night's sleep.

Here are a few things to think about:

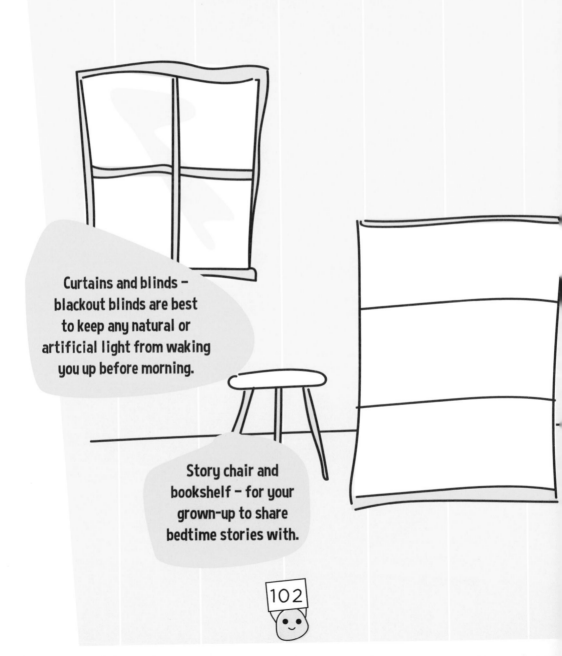

Curtains and blinds – blackout blinds are best to keep any natural or artificial light from waking you up before morning.

Story chair and bookshelf – for your grown-up to share bedtime stories with.

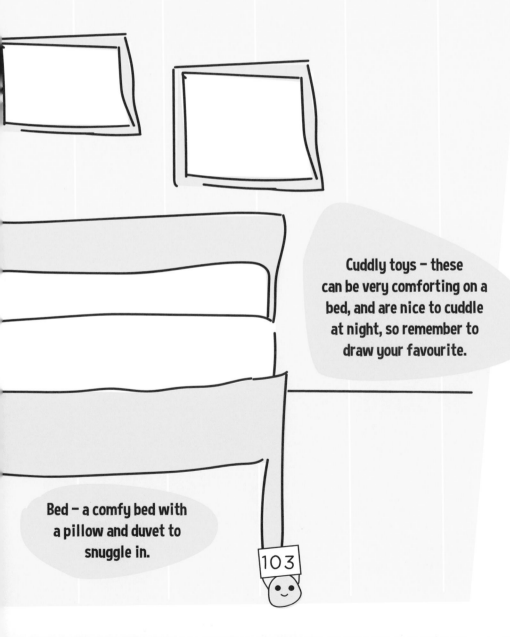

Bits and bobs – too many things can make a room look busy and cluttered, which will not help you get to sleep.

TV and gadgets – it's nice to have these in your chill-out pad, but make sure they're switched off an hour before bed, so find a place to store them out of sight!

Cuddly toys – these can be very comforting on a bed, and are nice to cuddle at night, so remember to draw your favourite.

Bed – a comfy bed with a pillow and duvet to snuggle in.

THIS PAGE WILL MAKE
YOU FALL ASLEEP

See if you can count all the sheep before you fall asleep!

TRY SOME OF THESE
SLEEPY PUZZLES

Help Kip to find his pillow

Complete the wordsearch

Dream
Doze
Nap
Rest
Snooze

t	p	c	a	d	r	n	i
e	d	r	e	a	m	p	q
c	o	n	x	m	u	a	k
e	z	o	o	n	s	p	y
f	e	t	p	j	l	w	n
a	w	q	s	m	o	r	p
r	l	n	c	e	t	x	a
o	v	e	p	w	r	m	n

106

Find the matching pair

Spot the 5 differences

Break it down

We now know what worry is and how it makes us feel and act. With a few tricks up our sleeves to help us cope with each stage of worry, we can break them down into small, manageable pieces.

Try these stepping stones the next time you feel worried:

Talk to my
favourite
grown-up

Break down
the worry into
smaller pieces

Challenge
each piece
one by one

**MY
WORRIES**

Allow the
feeling

Pause

Take
mindful
breaths

Smile

WORRY WORKSHEETS

Use the following pages to break down specific worries into smaller, more manageable pieces.

Write down your worry in the middle of the flower. Then, write down the things you can do to make that worry smaller or disappear within the petals.

The three-day "What if?" challenge

The things we worry about the most almost never happen. Just to prove this theory, let's test it out with the "What if?" challenge.

Over the next three days, start the day with your "What if?" worries for each day. It could look something like this:

Day 1

What if I don't do well in my test?

What if the person I'm paired with in science doesn't like me?

What if my grown-up forgets to pick me up?

What if I have nightmares?

DAY 1

What if...

☐

What if...

☐

What if...

☐

At the end of each day, go back over your "What ifs" and mark them with a tick if it really happened and a cross if it didn't happen.

What if...

What if...

What if...

Most of the things we care about in life involve uncertainty. We can't be sure we'll get the best marks for schoolwork, that everyone we meet will want to be our friend, that we'll always be healthy and strong. But we don't have to allow this uncertainty to stop us from living a happy life. Learning to embrace uncertainty rather than eliminate it is vital for our well-being.

DAY 3

_____

What if...
_____
_____ ☐

What if...
_____
_____ ☐

What if...
_____
_____ ☐

Now that you have completed the "What if?"
challenge, count up the number of ticks and crosses
and place the numbers in the boxes below.

DAY 1   DAY 2   DAY 3

✓ ☐ ✗ ☐   ✓ ☐ ✗ ☐   ✓ ☐ ✗ ☐

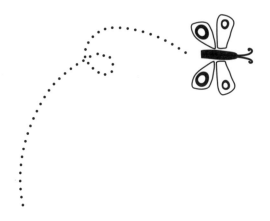

MY WORRY SHRINKER

Take a look back at your worry worksheets
and write a list of the things that help
you the most when worry strikes.

Once you have finished the list, you can
cut it out and keep it in a safe place to refer
to whenever you need it. Maybe make a few
copies so you can have one on your wall in
your bedroom and one in your school bag.

1

2

3

4

5

6

7

8

9

10

11

12

13

14

15

16

I can

123

Conclusion

It's not always possible to remove all worry from your mind, but using the skills learned in this book should go a long way to helping you feel more confident about facing your fears. Knowing that you can calm yourself when worry strikes is something that will be useful to you for your whole life, and the best part is, the more you do it the better you'll be!

There is no one better to be than myself.

My mistakes help me learn and grow.

I am an amazing person.

I forgive myself for my mistakes.

I have courage and confidence.

I am loved.

I deserve to be happy.

I can make a difference.

No matter how hard it is, I can do it.

I can be anything I want to be.

Today I am going to shine.

125

Answers

Pages 106–107

Help Kip to his pillow

Find the matching pair

Wordsearch

Spot the 5 differences

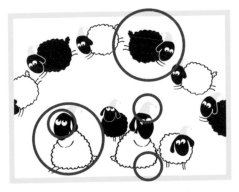

Final thoughts for parents and carers

Hopefully you and your child have been inspired by the fun activities in this book and your child can use their new-found skills to keep everyday worries in check.

Remember, there's no one-size-fits-all solution to worrying because every child and every human mind is different. Here are some final thoughts to consider:

- Aim to keep the lines of communication open with your child at all times, and talk through emotions, both the good and the bad. This way they will become better equipped to deal with normal levels of worry when it arises, and to know how to recognize and ask for help if it becomes overwhelming.

- If you feel that your child's worrying is having a negative effect on their daily life, it can be a good time to seek support outside the family. Start by talking to your child's school or doctor. They'll be able to advise the next steps. Alternatively, you could go directly to a therapist to discuss your concerns. Involve your child in decision-making, listen to any concerns they may have, validate and reassure them. Treat it just as you would if you were seeking help for a physical health symptom.

- Trust your own judgement if you feel the time is right to reach out for support, either for you or your child. Seeking support is a sign of strength and love, and you should never feel guilt or shame for doing so.

- When your child is struggling with worry, it can take a lot out of you. Make sure you as parents and carers have plenty of support, too. It can be hard to ask for help initially, but just know that those who care about you will want to be there for you.

Keep going — you're doing a wonderful job.

127

If you're interested in finding out more about our books,
find us on Facebook at Summersdale Publishers
and follow us on Twitter at @Summersdale.

www.summersdale.com

Image credits:

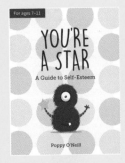